EVERYDAY NAMOKCOOK
매일 남옥 요리

TEN SIMPLE KOREAN RECIPES
열가지 간단한 한식 조리법

Recipes

Namok is my mother's name, and her food is my favorite.
Growing up, I was lucky to eat delicious home-cooked meals
from her, and her food set the standard of taste for me.
Her cooking did not always follow the traditional way, but she
created her Namok cooking. When I left South Korea and
began living alone in a foreign country, I started cooking the
dishes I missed. I tried to recall the food my mother had made
for me and re-created the meal in my way. Whether you are
in South Korea or overseas, the form of ingredients for Korean
food that you cook yourself is a little different, but you can
always create your unique taste.

There is a saying, 'son-mat,' which means that Korean dishes
are seasoned differently with the hands of the person cooking.
It often refers to the unique taste that comes from the hard work
and love of the person who makes it. Many people, including
many Koreans, say that cooking Korean food is complicated, yet
it is simple and healthy. You don't always have to follow the rules.
You can make Korean food at your local farmer's market with
just a few essential ingredients. I created this book hoping Korean
food will permeate your everyday life in a fun and easy way.

남옥은 제 엄마의 성함이고 엄마의 요리는 참 맛있습니다. 저는 운이 좋게도
맛있는 '집밥'을 먹고 자랐고, 그게 당연하다고 생각했어요. 그 음식들은 항상
전통적인 방식은 아니었지만 온전한 남옥요리였습니다. 그리고 저는 한국을
떠나 외국에서 혼자 살면서 스스로 그리운 요리를 해야 했습니다. 기억을
더듬으며 나만의 방식으로 나만의 남옥-집밥을 해먹었습니다. 국내든 해외든
직접 요리하는 한식 재료의 형태는 조금 다를 수 있지만, 한식은 언제나
자신만의 고유한 맛을 만들어 낼 수 있습니다.

한국 요리는 손으로 맛을 낸다는 '손맛'이라는 말이 있습니다. 음식을 만드는
사람의 노력과 사랑에서 나오는 독특한 맛 그리고 만들어 준 이의 정성이 담긴
음식 맛을 가리키는 말입니다. 요리하는 사람마다 각자의 손맛이 있습니다.
한국인을 포함한 많은 사람들이 한식을 만드는 과정이 복잡하다고 말하지만,
다른 관점에서 보면 한식은 간단하고 건강합니다. 항상 규칙을 따를 필요는
없습니다. 현지에서 몇 가지 기본 재료를 사서 충분히 요리할 수 있습니다.
여러분의 매일의 일상에 한식이 재미있고 자유롭게 스며들기를 바라며
이 책을 만들었습니다.

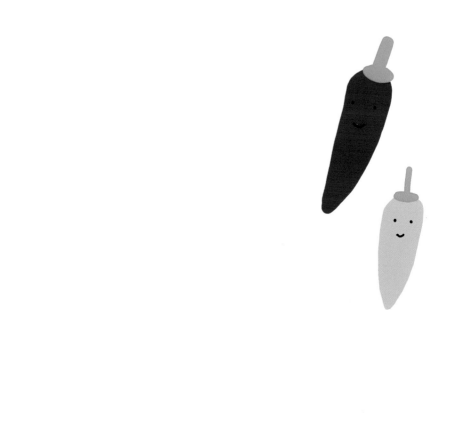

About Namok Cookbook
남옥 요리책 소개

Namok Cookbook is for everyday Korean homemade meals that are simple and easy to make. This book introduces all-time favorite home recipes with stories behind the delicious flavors.

이 책은 쉽고 간단한 한국 음식을 만들기 위한 가정식 요리책 입니다. 맛있는 요리 방법과 함께 음식에 따른 재미있는 민담과 그림을 소개합니다.

What is Hansik – Korean Cooking
한식

Korean meals generally consist of three main dishes. They are bap (steamed rice), guk (soup), and the main dish with meat, fish, or vegetables. They are also served with various banchan (side dishes).

일반적으로 한식은 세 가지 주요 요리로 구성됩니다. 밥, 국, 그리고 육류, 생선 또는 채소를 기본으로 한 메인 요리와 함께 다양한 반찬이 제공됩니다.

Ingredients in Korean Cooking
재료

These are the basic ingredients used in Korean kitchens.

Aekjeot
액젓

Aekjeot is a Korean fish sauce that brings out a more profound and robust aroma than other fish sauces. It is essential for making guk (Korean soup) or kimchi. For namok cook recipes, you can use any fish sauce you can get from a local supermarket.

Chamgirum
참기름

Chamgirum (roasted sesame oil) is a popular condiment in Korean cooking. Its delicious nutty fragrance is often added as the last touch for cooking to enhance the rich and nutty flavor (gosohan-mat). You can add chamgirum to various foods such as soup, rice, meat, and sauce. Koreans also enjoy deulgirum (perilla seed oil). We love it as much as chamgirum.

Doenjang
된장

Doenjang is an essential seasoning of Korean cooking and a representative ingredient of fermented soybean paste. It's similar to miso paste but more salty and savory. The use of doenjang is extensively varied. It is rich in dietary fiber, effective for nutrition control. In particular, traditional doenjang is suitable for removing harmful bacteria, carcinogens, and toxins. Doenjang also contains essential amino acids for the body, which helps to maintain a balanced diet.

Ganjang
간장

Ganjang (soy sauce) is made with meju (a brick of dried fermented soybeans), water, and salt. The method has been around since the Three Kingdoms period. In an onggi, a traditional Korean pot, add meju, water, and salt. The mixture is left for a few months outside in the cold winter. When the liquid becomes black, it is ready with an earthy, salty, and sweet taste. Korean ganjang tastes more nutritious and salty than Chinese/Japanese soy sauce.

Gochugaru
고추가루

Gochugaru, red chili powder or flakes, is used in many Korean dishes, either in spicy or mild-tasting dishes. And primarily, that's what makes Korean cooking spicy. Gochugaru is one of the essential Korean ingredients, and it is used in gochujang, kimchi, stews, soup, and various spicy dishes.

Gochujang
고추장

Gochujang is a Korean fermented red chili paste. It is made from a cultured soybean base called meju, combined with sun-dried red chili powder, rice powder, and salt. Meju tastes similar to doenjang (fermented soybean paste) or ganjang (soy sauce) in other countries. Gochujang is only used in Korean cooking and is a representative ingredient of Korean taste.

Kkae
깨

Roasted sesame seeds are as popular as chamgirum in Korean cooking. Roasted kkae is used as a garnish to add crunchiness and a nutty flavor. Koreans love to sprinkle kkae anywhere from bibimbap to kimchi to add the last touch of cooking.

tsp = 1 teaspoon = 5 milliliters
tbsp = 1 tablespoon = 15 milliliters

감자전

GAMJAJEON (RAINY DAY PANCAKES)

1

Gamjajeon (Rainy Day Pancakes) 감자전

Ingredients
(1-2 servings)

3-4 medium size potatoes
1 small golden onion
1/2 cup water
salt
cooking oil
1 green chili (optional)

Dipping sauce

1-2 tbsp ganjang (soy sauce)
1 tbsp vinegar
1 tsp kkae (roasted sesame seeds)

Gamjajeon is a typical dish on a rainy day in Korea.
It is a tradition to make a jeon (savory pancake) on rainy days.
The simple taste of gamja (potato) is suitable as a side dish for
a healthy meal or drink.

감자전은 비 오는 날의 대표적인 요리입니다. 한국에서는 비 오는 날이면
으레 전을 부쳐 먹는 관습이 있습니다. 단순한 재료의 맛으로 건강한 한 끼
식사 또는 음료 함께 주전부리로도 어울립니다.

1-3 Chop potatoes and onions into large chunks.

4-7 Grind potatoes and onions in a blender. Add water
    and salt before blending.

8   Prepare a strainer and a bowl.

9-11   Place the bowl under the filter and separate the
        solids and liquid for about 10 minutes. Then put the
        solids (potato and onion batter) in a separate bowl.
12-13   Check the potato starch in the bottom of the liquid.
        Discard the remaining juice.
14-16   Add the potato starch to the potato and onion batter
        mixture. Mix well.

17-23   Heat a frying pan with plenty of oil and cook the
            mixture over medium heat until golden brown.
24   Decorate with a slice of green chili if desired.
            Serve with ganjang dipping sauce.

비빔밥

HARMONY BiBiMBAP

2

Harmony Bibimbap 비빔밥

Ingredients	2 bowls of steamed rice
(2 servings)	2 eggs
	salt
	pepper
	cooking oil
	chamgirum (roasted sesame oil)
	1 tbsp ganjang (soy sauce) for beef
	70g spinach
	70g mung bean or soybean sprouts
	40g mushrooms (any kind)
	1/2 carrot
	1/2 zucchini
	70g ground beef
Sauce	1-2 tbsp gochujang (red chili paste)
	2 tbsp chamgirum (roasted sesame oil)
	1 tbsp kkae (roasted sesame seeds)
	1/2 tbsp apple or rice vinegar (optional)
	1/2 tsp honey or sugar (optional)

Bibimbap is one of the representative Korean dishes. Bibimbap means mixing (bibim) steamed rice (bap). To make bibimbap, mix rice with meat, assorted vegetables, eggs, and seasonings such as gochujang (red chili paste) and chamgirum (roasted sesame oil). The harmony of ingredients and aroma creates a healthy and tasty meal.

비빔밥은 대표적인 한국 요리 중 하나로, 밥과 나머지 재료를 함께 비벼 먹는다는 뜻입니다. 쌀밥에 고기나 다양한 채소, 달걀 등과 고추장, 참기름 등의 양념을 넣고 섞어 먹습니다. 모든 재료의 맛과 향의 조화가 독특하고 건강한 맛을 만듭니다.

1-3   Stir fry shredded carrots on medium-high to high heat with a sprinkle of cooking oil, and season with salt and pepper.

4-6   Stir fry sliced zucchini on medium-high to high heat with a sprinkle of cooking oil, and season with salt and pepper.

7-8   Stir fry ground beef on medium-high to high heat with a sprinkle of cooking oil, and season with ganjang.

9-11   Stir fry mushrooms on medium-high to high
        heat with a sprinkle of cooking oil, and season with
        salt and pepper.
12-14   Stir fry bean sprouts on medium-high to high heat
        with a few drops of water. Add some cooking oil
        when cooked halfway through, and season with salt
        and pepper.
15-16   Bring water to a boil in a pot and blanch spinach
        until soft.

17-18	Prepare a fried egg per serving.
19-20	Prepare a bowl of steamed rice per serving.
21-24	Place all the toppings and sauce on top of the rice and add a drizzle of chamgirum. Mix well to create a delicious meal of the day.

잔치국수

JANCHI GUKSU (LONG LiFE NOODLE)

3

Janchi Guksu (Long Life Noodle) 잔치국수

Ingredients (2 servings)	200g somyeon noodles for 2 (thin white noodles)
Broth	1 liter water
	2-3 dried anchovies
	2-3 dried shrimps (optional)
	10g dashima (dried kelp)
	1 tbsp ganjang (soy sauce)
	salt
Gomyeong (garnish)	1/3 zucchini
	1/3 gim (dried seaweed paper)
	1 eggs for jidan (thin egg sheets)
Sauce	1 tbsp ganjang (soy sauce)
	1 tsp green onion
	1/2 tsp chamgirum (roasted sesame oil)
	1/2 tsp minced garlic
	1 tsp kkae (roasted sesame seeds)
	pepper

Janchi guksu or banquet noodles is a traditional Korean dish for celebratory occasions such as wedding receptions and 60th birthday parties. It is a warm and savory soup with long, thin white somyeon noodles, which symbolizes a wish for a long life. A mouthful of warmth adds a touch of perfection on a happy day.

잔치국수는 한국의 전통적인 잔치 요리 중 하나입니다. 길고 얇은 국수 가락처럼 오래 잘 살라는 의미에서 유래되어 오늘날에도 결혼식, 생일잔치, 환갑잔치 등의 축하 행사에서 국수를 먹는 관습이 있습니다. 따뜻한 육수와 곁들인 면과 채소 고명이 어우러져 몸을 따뜻하고 편안하게 합니다.

1-5   Add minced garlic, chamgirum, pepper, sliced green onion, kkae into ganjang. Mix well.

6-7	Add 1 liter of water to a pot. Add dasima, dried anchovies, and dried shrimp (optional). Bring to the boil.
8	On low heat, simmer for 20 minutes. Do not cover with a lid; otherwise, the fish smell will remain in the stock.
9	Remove all ingredients from the soup.
10	Let it boil once again and season with soy sauce and salt.

11-18   For jidan, crack an egg into a bowl. Add some salt, and beat gently. Preheat a pan and add very little cooking oil. Cook a thin sheet over low heat without browning it. After cooling the jidan completely, cut it gently into thin strips.

19-20 Finely chop zucchini. Stir fry on medium-high to high heat with a sprinkle of cooking oil.

21-22 Bring water to the boil and add somyeon.

23 Stir gently with chopsticks to prevent the noodles from sticking to each other.

24-25 Add cold water about 2-3 times whenever the pot overflows to add some texture.

26 Put the cooked noodles in a sieve and rinse them in cold water. Be careful of hot water while draining.

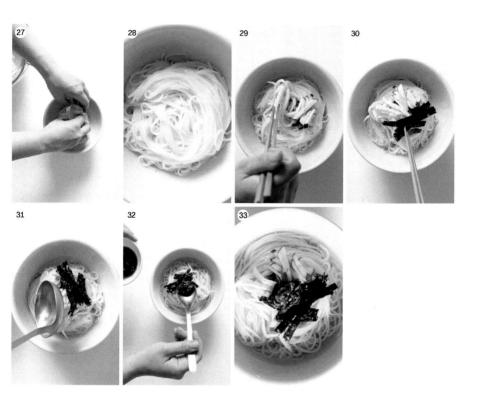

27-28   Put the cooked noodles in a bowl.
29-30   Garnish with stir-fried zucchini, egg jidan, and some gim.
31   Add hot soup over the bowl of noodles and garnish
             carefully.
32   Add some sauce as preferred.
33   Serve warm.

양배추 쌈밥과 두부쌈장

SSAMBAP (FORTUNE RICE) AND DUBU SSAMJANG

4

SSambap and Dubu Ssamjang 양배추 쌈밥과 두부쌈장

Ingredients
(2 servings)

1/2 small cabbage
salt

2 bowls of steamed rice

dubu ssamjang (tofu sauce):
1/2 dubu (tofu)
1 tsp ganjang (soy sauce)
1-2 tsp doenjang/miso
(fermented soybean paste)
1-2 tsp gochujang (red chili paste)
1/2 stalk of sliced or minced green onion
1 tbsp chopped onion
2 tbsp honey or sugar
1 tbsp kkae (roasted sesame seeds)
2 tbsp chamgirum (roasted sesame oil)
1/2 tsp minced garlic

a cotton cloth

Ssambap means rice wrapped in vegetable leaves. 'Ssam' means to wrap something, and 'bap' means steamed rice. Either fresh or lightly cooked vegetable leaves are good. Ssam is a food with the meaning of 'eating wrapped luck,' which symbolizes praying for good luck. On the first full moon of the year, on Daeboreum Day, there is a tradition of blessing the moon, a symbol of abundance and eating ssam to pray for good fortune. It is served with ssamjang sauce, a mixture of doenjang and gochujang.

쌈밥은 잎에 싸인 쌀밥을 의미합니다. 쌈에 사용되는 다양한 채소의 잎은 신선하게 생으로 먹거나 가볍게 익혀 먹습니다. 쌈은 '무엇을 감싸다'라는 뜻을 가지고 있습니다. 쌈은 '복(福)을 싸서 먹는다'라는 의미가 담긴 음식이며, 복을 기원하는 상징성을 부여하고 있습니다. 한해 첫 보름달이 뜨는 명절, 대보름날에는 풍요로움의 상징인 달을 축복하고 풍요를 위해 복을 기원하며 쌈을 먹는 전통이 있습니다. 된장과 고추장 그리고 약간의 향신료를 기본으로 만든 장을 함께 곁들여 먹습니다.

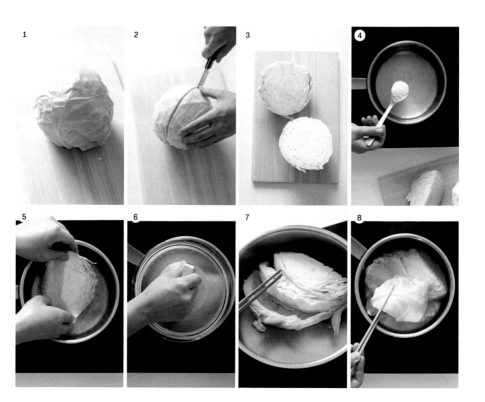

1-8   Cut a head of cabbage and cook it in boiled water.
Add salt for flavor. Cover the lid and cook it on high
heat for about 5 minutes. Turn it over. Continue
to cook it for another 8-10 minutes until the cabbage
turns soft and transparent.

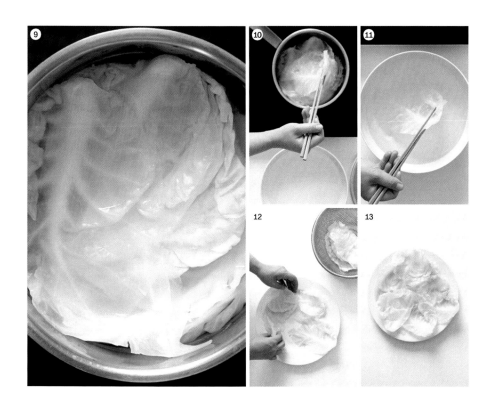

9-13   Rinse it with cold water. Wait until the cabbage
        becomes cool.

14-18   Wrap dubu with a clean cloth. Squeeze out all the liquid from the dubu. Place dubu in a bowl.

19-22   Prepare minced garlic, chopped onion, and sliced green onion.
23-26   Add onion, garlic, green onion, doenjang or miso, gochujang, kkae, honey, or sugar in the bowl of squeezed dubu. Mix well.

27-31   Unfold a cabbage sheet. Add an appropriate amount of rice, and wrap it in bite-size pieces.

32-33   Put dubu ssamjang on top of cabbage ssambap before serving.

미역국

MIYEOKGUK (BIRTHDAY SOUP)

5

50   Miyeokguk (Birthday soup) 미역국

Ingredients
(2-3 servings)

15g miyeok (dried brown seaweed/wakame)
60g beef (optional)

1 liter of water

1/2 tsp minced garlic
2-3 tbsp chamgirum (roasted sesame oil)
2-3 tbsp ganjang (soy sauce)
salt

Everyone has a bowl of warm miyeokguk on a birthday morning in Korea. Miyeokguk is a memory for our parents, and we thank them for giving us such a beautiful life. Also, the main ingredient, miyeok (brown seaweed/wakame), is known for containing nutrients that are good for mothers who have just given birth to a child. It is a warm bowl of life and love by parents, usually served with a bowl of rice.

미역국은 주 재료인 미역을 끓여낸 국으로, 생일을 기념하고 낳아주신 부모님께 감사를 드리는 의미로 생일날 먹습니다. 미역국은 아이를 낳은 산모에게도 애용되는 음식입니다. 해초에 함유된 영양소는 몸의 회복에 도움이 되고 유익하며 건강한 맛과 영양이 풍부합니다. 주로 쌀밥 그리고 반찬과 함께 곁들여 먹습니다.

1-4   Prepare dried miyeok and soak it in a large bowl
for about 30 minutes while allowing it to expand.
It will swell about ten times bigger.

5-7   Cut beef into bite-sized pieces.

8   Prepare minced garlic.

9-13   Stir-fry garlic and beef over medium heat with chamgirum until lightly cooked.

14-15   Drain water and rinse the miyeok a couple of times under running water. If you're using non-pre-cut miyeok, cut it with scissors or a knife to about 3-5 centimeters.

16   Add the soaked miyeok into the pot with garlic, and beef, and stir-fry over low-medium heat for about 3 minutes.

17-21   Add water. Add ganjang and salt (if needed). Bring to a boil over medium-high heat until the meat has fully cooked, about 10 to 15 minutes.

22-24   Serve warm in a bowl with rice and other Korean side dishes.

김치 비빔국수

KiMCHi BiBiM GUKSU (SUMMER TiME NOODLES)

Ingredients (2 servings)	200g somyeon noodles for 2 (thin white noodles) 1 boiled egg
kimchi bibim sauce	40g kimchi 2 tbsp kkae (roasted sesame seeds) 4 tbsp chamgirum (roasted sesame oil) 1 tbsp gochujang (red chili paste) 1-2 tsp honey or sugar 1 tsp vinegar 1 tsp ganjang (soy sauce) (optional)

Bibimguksu is a signature Korean dish along with bibimbap, and it is a symbol of bibim (mix) culture in Korean cooking. This fresh noodle dish is popular on a hot summer day. It is garnished with kimchi, vegetables, gim (dried seaweed paper), meat, and eggs.

비빔국수는 비빔밥과 함께 한식의 비빔 문화를 상징하는 음식으로 계절과 기호에 따라 다양하게 즐길 수 있는 국수 요리입니다. 입맛 없는 여름날, 가볍게 비벼 먹는 한 끼 식사로 기호에 맞는 달걀, 김, 고기, 채소, 김치 등의 고명을 함께 곁들여 먹습니다.

1-3   Prepare chopped kimchi and place it in a bowl.

4-8   Add vinegar, honey or sugar, gochujang, chamgirum, and kkae.

9-10   Mix well and add some ganjang if needed.
11-13   Bring water to the boil and add somyeon. Stir gently
        to prevent the noodles from sticking to each other.
14-16   Put the cooked noodles in a sieve and rinse them
        in cold water. Be careful of hot water while draining.

17-18 Drain water from the noodles.
19-20 Serve in a bowl.
21-24 Garnish with kimchi bibim sauce, chamgirum, kkae, and half of a boiled egg.

떡국

TTEOKGUK (HAPPY NEW YEAR SOUP)

7

Tteokguk (Happy New Year Soup) 떡국

Ingredients (1–2 servings)	800 liters of water 400g tteokguk-tteok (coin-shaped rice cake) 1/2 tsp minced garlic 3 tbsp chamgirum (roasted sesame oil) 2-3 tbsp ganjang (soy sauce) salt pepper
Gomyeong (garnish)	150-200g brisket or sirloin steak beef 1 jidan (thin egg sheets) 1/3 gim (dried seaweed paper) 1 tbsp chopped green onion

Tteokguk is a traditional Korean New Year's food that wishes a happy new year. The long and white tteok (rice cake) means longevity and purity. A coin-shaped tteok symbolizes wealth. A bowl of rice cake soup (tteokguk) is tasty and contains wisdom of our ancestors to wish for a happy new year with a sincere heart from a clean, simple, and reverent spirit.

새해 첫날에는 복을 기원하며 떡국을 먹는 풍습이 있습니다. 하얀 가래떡의 순백의 색감은 순수를, 긴 모양은 장수를, 동그랗게 썰은 모양은 부유를 기원했다고 합니다. 떡국은 화려하지 않으면서 정갈하고 소박한 그리고 경건한 마음으로 새해를 맞이하고픈 선인들의 지혜가 담겨있다고 합니다.

1-2   Prepare chopped green onion.
3-5   To make jidan, separate egg white and yolk into two
       different bowls. Add some salt. Beat each of them
       without creating foam.

6-10   Preheat a pan and add very little cooking oil. Cook thin sheets without browning them over low heat.

11-12   After cooling the jidan completely, gently cut them into thin strips.

13   Cut some gim into thin strips. It is easier with scissors.

14   Prepare tteokguk-tteok.
15   Soak it in water for at least 10 minutes, then drain it.
16-18   Cut beef into small bite-sized pieces.

19-21   Stir-fry the beef over medium-high heat with chamgirum.

22-23   When the beef is half cooked, add minced garlic. Add ganjang, a pinch of salt, and pepper.

24-28	Add about 250-300 ml of water, cover the lid and bring to a simmer. Cook for 20 to 30 minutes over medium heat until the beef is tender and infused with flavor. Place the meat into a bowl.
29	Preheat a pot over medium heat and add a few drops of chamgirum.
30	Add about 400-500 ml of water.
31	Once the water boils, add cooked beef. Leave some meat for garnish later.

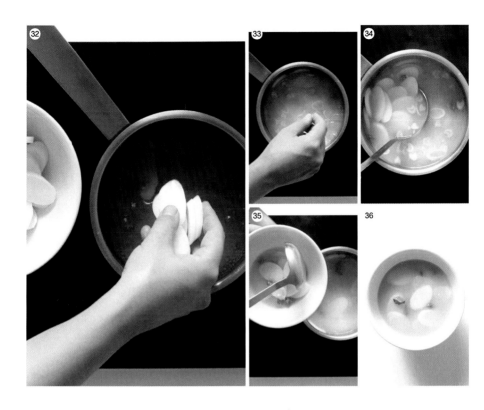

| 32-35 | Add tteok and green onion. Cook for about 3-5 minutes until the tteok is thoroughly cooked and soft. Be careful not to overcook the tteok as they can become mushy. Add salt if necessary. |
| 36 | Serve in a bowl. |

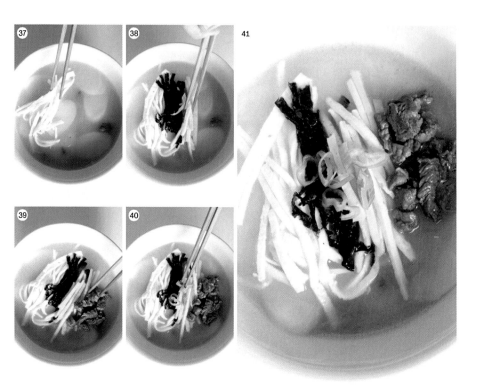

37-41   Add all prepared gomyeong (garnish) on top of
         tteokguk. Serve a warm bowl of tteokguk with kimchi
         and other Korean side dishes.

불고기

BULGOGi
(FiRE BEEF)

8

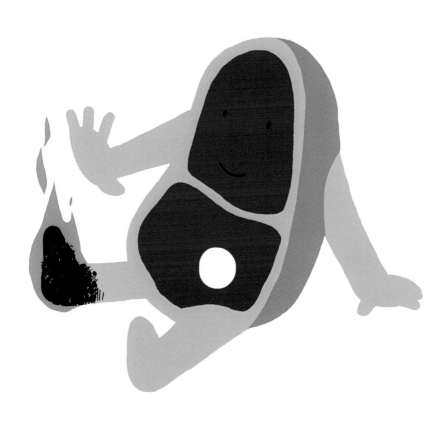

Bulgogi (Fire Beef) 불고기

Ingredients
(2 servings)

300g thinly sliced beef
1/2 sliced onion
1 sliced carrot
1 stalk of green onion

Sauce

200-250 ml water
1 pear or apple
1/2 onion
1-3 cloves of garlic
3 tbsp brown sugar
3-4 tbsp ganjang (soy sauce)
2 tbsp cooking wine
3 tbsp chamgirum (roasted sesame oil)
salt
black pepper

Garnish

1 tsp kkae (roasted sesame seeds)

Bulgogi is a traditional sweet and tender barbeque dish that has been around in Korea for thousands of years. Bulgogi has been famous as a staple food for banquets for a long time. Bulgogi is thinly sliced beef marinated in ganjang (soy sauce). It is either char-grilled or stir-fried in a pan. You can add various vegetables or noodles as desired. Bulgogi is good with a bowl of rice and fresh vegetables.

불고기는 한국에서 수천 년 전부터 먹어온 전통 음식으로, 보통 얇게 저민 소고기를 간장 소스에 재웠다가 구워 먹는 요리입니다. 이 음식은 선조들의 다양한 지혜가 담긴 요리로, 예로부터 잔칫상에 단골 음식으로 인기가 많았습니다. 불고기는 양념된 고기를 불에 구워, 부드럽고 달콤한 맛이 일품입니다. 기호에 따라 여러 가지 채소나 면을 추가해 먹기도 하며, 보통은 밥과 신선한 채소와 함께 먹습니다.

1   Prepare thinly sliced beef in a large bowl.
2-5   Sprinkle brown sugar over each layer.

6-9   Cut a pear or an apple into small pieces. Remove the core.

9-10   Cut an onion into small pieces.

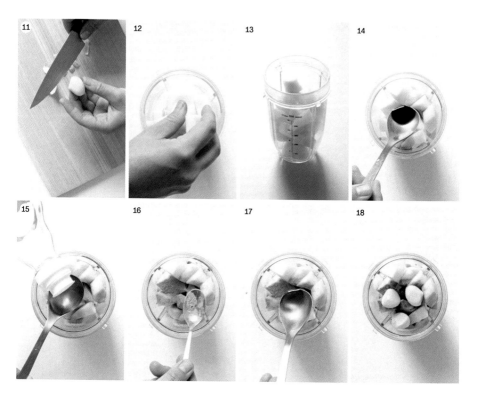

11　　　　Peel garlic.
12-13　　Add pear, onion, and garlic to a blender.
14-18　　Add ganjang, cooking wine, pepper, chamgirum,
　　　　　and a sprinkle of salt (optional).

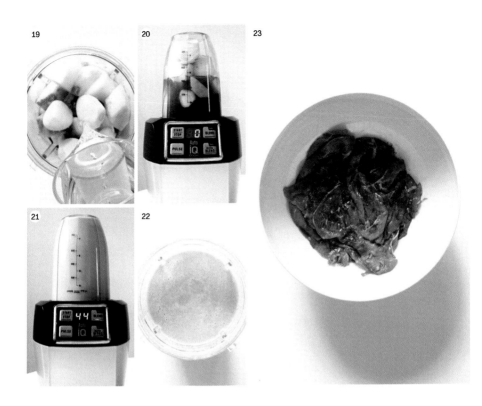

19-22   Add some water and blend all the ingredients.
                  And blend until it becomes smooth.

23   Marinated beef.

24-28   Add the blended sauce to the bowl with marinated beef. Mix well with utensils or hands. Keep it in the refrigerator for at least 20 minutes (the meat will become more tender and flavorful).

29-30   Slice onion and green onion.
31-32   Add sliced onion and green onion to the bowl
             of beef.
33-34   Preheat the pan on medium-high heat and
             add all the ingredients in the bowl to the pan.
             Stir gently to untangle the meat.
35-36   Slice some carrots and add them to the pan.

37-38   Cook for 20 to 30 minutes on medium to high heat until the meat is cooked thoroughly and the vegetables are soft.

39-41   Place bulgogi on a plate and garnish it with some kkae. Serve it with a bowl of steamed rice, noodles, or other side dishes.

Bulgogi (Fire Beef) 불고기

무생채

MUSAENG CHAE (KiMCHi RADiSH SALAD)

9

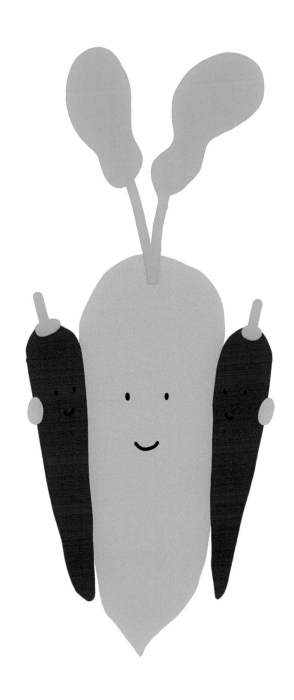

Musaengchae (Kimchi Radish Salad) 무생채

Ingredients (2 servings)	1/2 medium-sized radish
Sauce	1-2 tbsp gochugaru (red pepper powder) 2 tbsp honey or sugar 2 tbsp apple or rice vinegar 1 tbsp aekjeot or fish sauce 2 tbsp kkae (roasted sesame seeds) 1 tsp minced garlic 1-2 tsp salt 1/2 stalk of sliced green onion
For serving	chamgirum (roasted sesame oil) kkae (roasted sesame seeds)

Musaengchae is a freshly shredded radish salad dish seasoned with vinegar, sugar, and gochugaru (red chili powder). It can be a quick alternative to kimchi. For white (non-spicy) musaengchae, add garlic, fish sauce, sugar, and vinegar. It tastes good, served cold, crisp, and fresh, and goes well with various dishes.

무생채는 간단하고 쉬운 샐러드처럼 먹는 김치로 가늘게 채 썬 무에 소금, 식초, 다진 파, 마늘, 설탕 그리고 고운 고춧가루 등의 양념을 넣고 새콤달콤하게 무쳐 먹는 반찬입니다. 같은 재료에 고춧가루를 넣지 않고 식초만을 사용하여 하얗게 무쳐 먹는 방법도 있습니다. 아삭하고 신선한 맛으로 차갑게 보관하여 다양한 음식과 함께 즐기기 좋습니다.

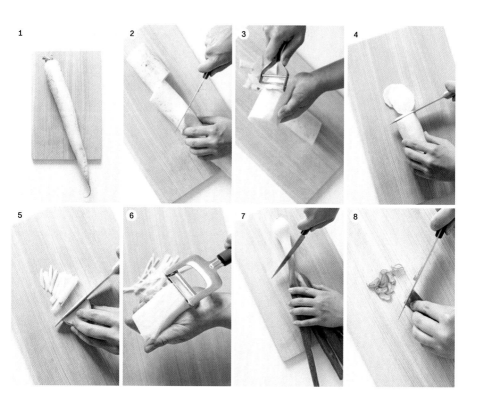

1-6   Peel the radish and cut into the appropriate size.
Slice it thinly, then shred it. You can use
a julienne cutter to make the process easier.

7-8   Chop green onion.

      Musaengchae (Kimchi Radish Salad) 무생채

9-16   Place shredded radish in a bowl and add aekjeot or
fish sauce, salt, honey (sugar), vinegar, garlic, ginger,
gochugaru (red chili powder).

17-18   Add green onion and kkae.

19-21   Mix all ingredients thoroughly and add more aekjeot
         or fish sauce for more saltiness if desired.

22-24   Place musaengchae over a bowl of steamed rice, or
         you can serve it on a plate as a side dish. Add
         chamgirum and kkae before serving. Musaengchae
         stays fresh for about 3-4 days in an airtight
         container in the refrigerator.

JANG KIMCHI (KING'S KIMCHI)

Jang Kimchi (King's Kimchi) 장김치

Ingredients

Sauce

300 ml whole cane sugar
300 ml rice or apple vinegar
300 ml ganjang (soy sauce)

Vegetables and fruits

1/2 napa cabbage
1/2 radish
1/2 lotus root
1/2 carrot
1/2 cucumber
1/2 onion
1/2 pear
1-2 celery stalk
1-3 garlic cloves

Add your favorite vegetables, fruits, and nuts

1-2 any food container (sterilized)

Unlike the well-known vivid red and spicy Kimchi you know, Jangkimchi has a calm and unique color. The sweetness of ganjang (soy sauce) adds an exceptional touch with a simple taste. Various vegetables such as cabbage, radish, lotus root, and carrots are pickled with ganjang. The seasoning for jangkimchi doesn't include jeotgal (salted fish), salt, or red peppers, so it is easy on the stomach. Long ago, it was only made for royals in the palace.

장김치는 다양한 채소와 과일 그리고 견과류를 단맛을 더한 간장에 절여 담그는 김치입니다. 장김치는 궁중에서 먹었던 음식으로 다양한 고급스러운 재료를 사용합니다. 양념에 젓갈이나 고춧가루 그리고 소금 또한 사용되지 않아 섭취 시 부담이 없습니다. 상차림에 곁들여 먹기에 쉽고 다양한 음식들과 잘 어울립니다.

1-13   Clean and then cut the vegetables and fruits into the
desired size.

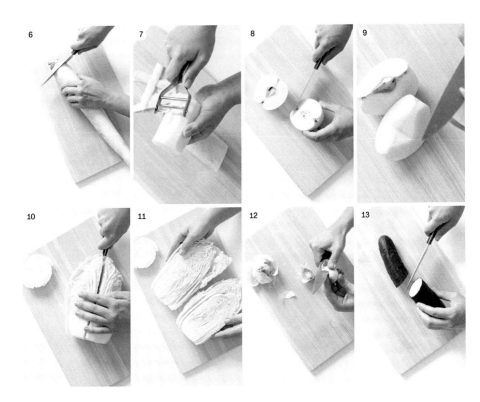

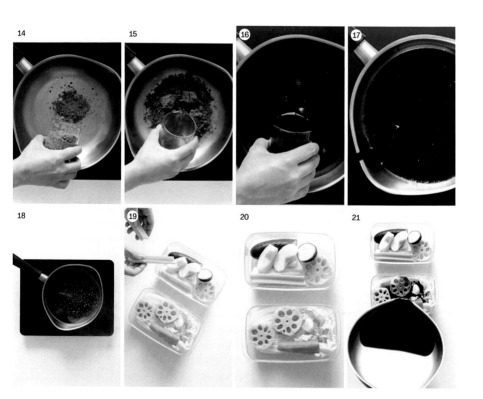

14-18   Add sugar, vinegar, and ganjang to a pan and boil over medium-high heat. Turn off the heat.

19-20   Place vegetables and fruits in sterilized containers.

21   Add sauce over vegetables and fruits while the sauce is still hot. The heat will make them crunchy.

25   26

22-24   Cool them completely before putting the lids on.
         Keep them at room temperature for a day, and then
         keep them in the refrigerator for at least a day
         before serving.
25-26   Enjoy the taste of jangkimchi that changes every day.
         Jangkimchi can be stored for up to 2 months in the
         refrigerator.

27-31 Cut jangkimchi into bite-sized pieces before
serving. Jangkimchi goes well with steamed rice,
noodles, meat, or fish. Also, the sauce can be used
as a salad dressing or mixed with water for a hot/
cold soup. Jangkimchi will stimulate your appetite
and brighten your meal.

EVERYDAY NAMOKCOOK
매일 남옥 요리

TEN SIMPLE KOREAN RECIPES
열가지 간단한 한식 조리법

Author
Layuhl Jang
장지윤

Illustration / Hand writing
Martijn in't Veld
HappyPotatoPress

Photography
Michele Foti

Editing / Design
Anita Poltronieri
Marcello Jacopo Biffi

Proofreader
Jihei C

Second Edition
500 copies

Printed in Italy by
Ancora Arti Grafiche

ISBN
979-12-210-2772-3